Prayers for Growing and Other Pains: More Family Prayers

By Pat Corrick Hinton

Winston Press

Photographs by:
Rick Smolan—p. 89; Robert J. Cunningham—p. 13; Cyril A. Reilly—
pp. 48, 80; John Maines—p. 21; Jean-Claude Lejeune—pp. 19, 30;
John Arms—pp. 8, 38, 58; Vernon Sigl—p. 42.

The Scripture text on page 74 is taken from *The New English Bible*, copyright © 1961, 1970 by the delegates of the Oxford University Press and the syndics of the Cambridge University Press. Reprinted by permission. All other Scripture texts used in this work are taken from the *New American Bible*, copyright © 1970 by the Confraternity of Christian Doctrine, Washington, D.C. Used by permission of the copyright owner. All rights reserved.

Copyright © 1981, Pat Corrick Hinton
Library of Congress Catalog Card Number: 81-50554
ISBN: 0-86683-603-9
Printed in the United States of America

All rights reserved. No part of this book may be reproduced or used in any form without written permission from Winston Press, Inc.

5 4 3 2 1

Winston Press, Inc.
430 Oak Grove
Minneapolis, Minnesota 55403

To my mother,
who first
taught me to pray

Contents

Introduction 6

Where Do I Begin?
Beginning 9
Morning 10
Blessing 11
Busyness 12
Dependence 14
Forgiveness 15
Blindness 16
Acceptance 17
Care 18
Evening 20

Why Me, Lord?
Monotony 24
Bewilderment 25
Braces 26
Weariness 27
Working 28
Dieting 29
Moods 31
Loneliness 33
Worry 34
Pain 36

Where Can I Find God?
Discovery 39
Freeway 41
Song from the North Woods 43
Creation 45
Awareness 46
Backyard 47
Color 49
St. Therese 51

Search 52
Death 54

Where in the World Are We Growing?
Risk 56
Trust 57
Family 59
Rush 61
Choices 62
Hope 64
Gift 65
Progress 66
Worship 67
Values 68

Who Is Jesus, Anyway?
Question 70
Person 71
Outdoorsman 72
Free 73
Prayerful 74
Powerful 75
Wondering 76
Friend 78
Present 81
Successful 82

Does My Light Shine?
Lent 84
Fasting 85
Holy Week 86
Kingdom 87
Easter 88
Spring 90
Gratitude 92
Holy Spirit 94
Peace 95

Introduction

This is a book about the everydayness of God. In writing these prayers and reflections, I have tried to take an honest look at the feelings that many of us experience in the problems and challenges of being followers of Jesus. I have attempted to convey joy as well as frustration, awe as well as boredom, celebration as well as pain. The feelings expressed here, both positive and negative, always maintain a sense of God's constant, loving Presence.

In *Prayer After Nine Rainy Days* I emphasized building an attitude of prayer on the child's natural state of wonder. As we grow up and older this attitude of wonder should grow too. Jesus never lost his sense of wonder at the enormous goodness of his Father. If we are following him, we will wonder at how we ourselves grow and change. We will wonder at how very generous God is in his gifts to us. Especially will we wonder at his faithfulness to us every day, through the ups and downs of our uniquely ordinary lives. As we realize more and more that our God is truly with us, we discover our own need to make more room for him, to search out his Presence in everyday situations.

I hope the words in this book will help to point out his loving Presence in our lives and encourage us to respond to him with words of our own in love and faithfulness. "I will never forget you. See, upon the palms of my hands I have written your name"   Isaiah 49:16.

Where Do I Begin?

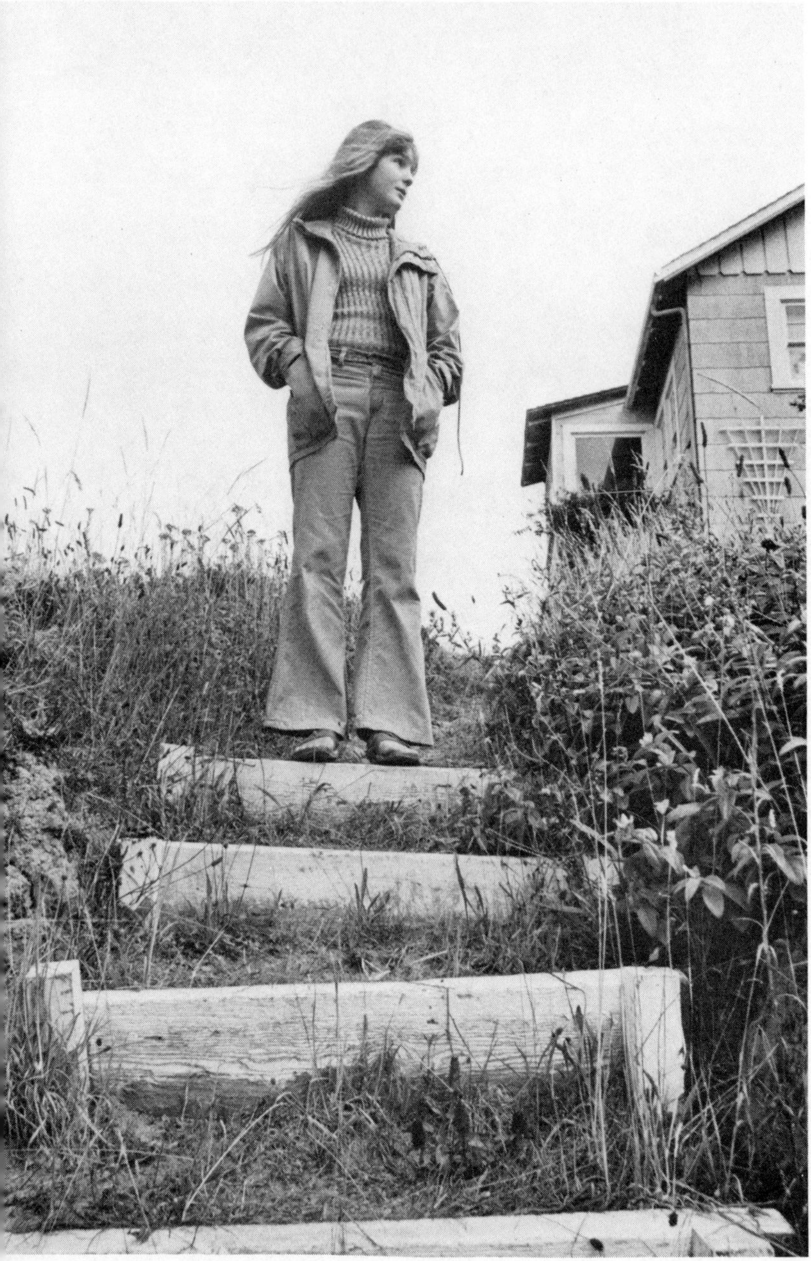

Beginning

God, our Father,
bless this beginning.

It's fresh and new
like your love each morning.

Today is your
new mercy
to me —
a new chance,
a new challenge,
a new path,
untried, uncut.

I want to walk it with you.

I want it to be
the first
of many new beginnings
entrusted to you.

Morning

Loving Father,
thank you for a night of rest
and for the gift of this
new day.

We thank you for being with us
to give meaning
to what we do.

Thank you for loving us
and for giving us
courage
to share your love
with those we meet today.

Amen.

Blessing

God, our Father,
we thank you for this day,
for the gift of life
and for the food
we are about to eat.

Thank you for providing us
with what we need
and for giving us each other.

Please bless all
whom we love
and keep us close to you.

We ask this through Jesus.

Amen.

Busyness

Loving Father,
these are busy days
for us.

We thank you
for gifting us
with talents and abilities
that keep us busy.

We pray for those
who are bored
or think they have
too much time.

Please help us see your Presence
in our activity.

Inspire us
with good ideas
and loving hearts.

Let us see you
in all we do.

We ask this in the name of Jesus.

Amen.

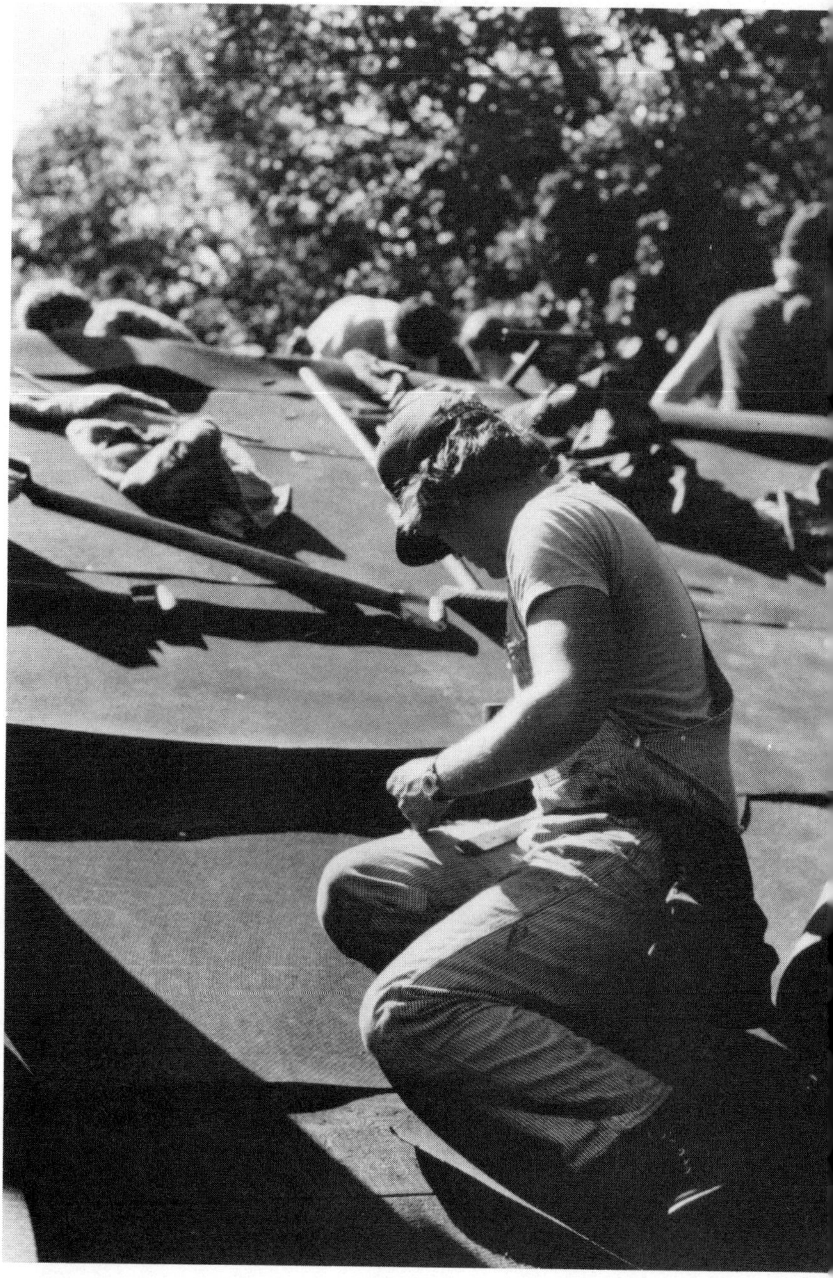

Dependence

Holy Spirit,
I have so much to do today
that I don't know where to begin.

So I'm handing the day over to you.

I'm depending on you
to guide me
from project to project.

Show me what to do and when to do it.

Please take away
my jitters and anxiety
and replace them
with your own Spirit
of love and completeness.

I ask that I might do this
with peace
in the name of Jesus.

Amen.

Forgiveness

Forgive me, loving Father,
for my failure to love.

I am sorry
that to save my pride
I hurt someone I care about.
I am sorry
that in taking care of
my own feelings first
I was insensitive to those
around me.
I am sorry
that — though I want to be honest —
I don't always tell the truth.

Forgive me, Father,
as I forgive anyone
who has failed to love me.

I want to change.
I want to be healed.
I want to live in
your sunlight,
not in spite of my
being human,
but because I am so very human.

Blindness

Lord,
what can I do
to remember
your constant love?

When I'm flat on my face
with frustration
or failure,
I might remember
"Help!"

When the day is glorious
and I'm sailing high,
feeling free
and full of courage,
I might remember
"Thanks!"

But why do I forget you
in the nuts and bolts
and the daily grind?

Why don't I see you
in what's ordinary?

Would you give me
a mud patch
that would open my eyes?

Acceptance

God, our loving Father,
thank you
for letting me come to you
as I am.

Some days
my idea of service
is to take care of
only me.

I am sorry for those days,
but I give them to you
because they are
part of me.

Thank you for loving me
as I am,
for appreciating whatever
I have to offer you
whether great or small.

Thank you for accepting
my readiness
to serve you
and for not expecting me
to be a superstar.

Thank you
for letting me
be me.

Care

Loving Father,
you are so good.

Sometimes you provide
an answer
before we can put
the question
into words.

Never for an instant
do you forget us
and our many needs.

You hold us in the
palm of your hand.

You cherish and guide us.
Truly you love us.
We are gifted people.

19

Evening

God, our Father,
as this day ends
I praise you
for all my gifts,
and I praise you
for all my problems.

I felt you were
with me today
especially....

Thank you
for the times
when I recognized your Presence.
I am sorry
for the moments
when my problems
got the best of me.

I ask you to heal
my failings and selfishness.

I look forward
with peace and joy
to a new day with you
tomorrow.

I ask this through
Jesus, your Son
and my Brother.

Amen.

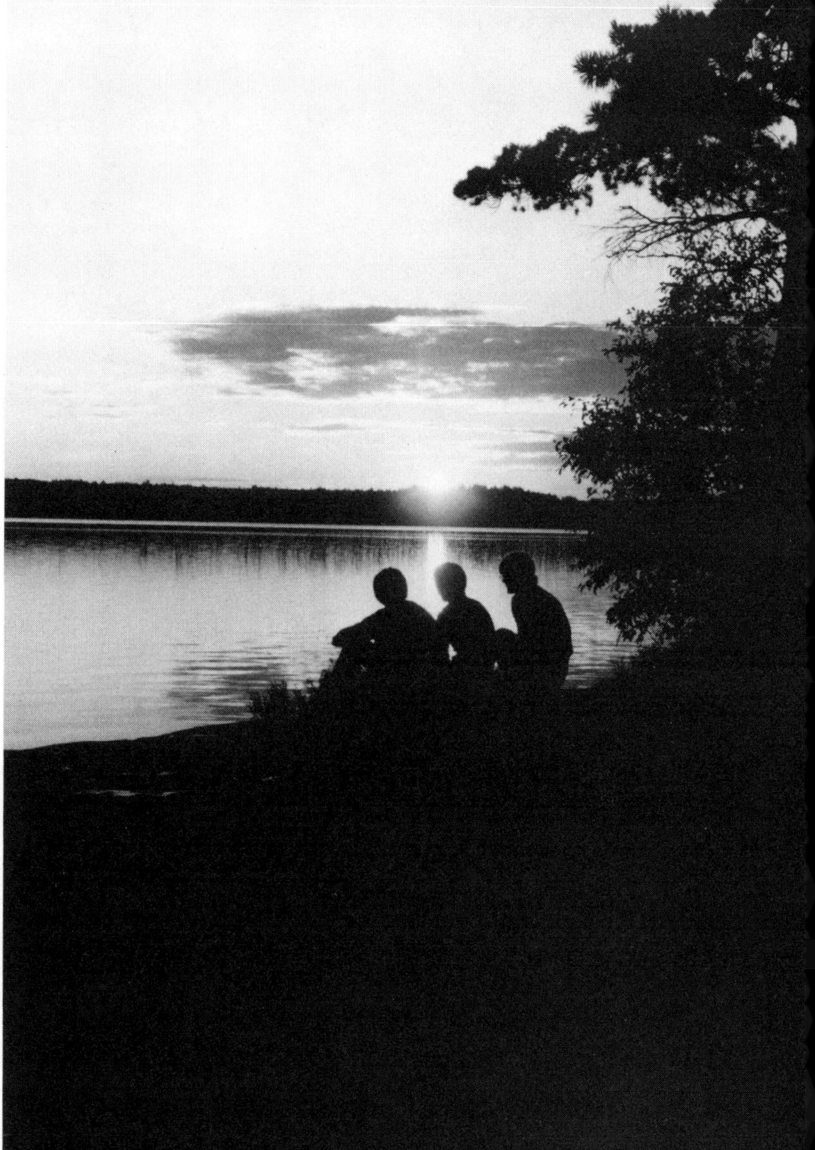

Why Me, Lord?

Monotony

Loving Father,
I'm thanking you
for this day.

I'm thanking you
for all the good things
that must be happening
even though I'm too bored
to figure out
what those good things are.

By thanking you,
I remind myself
that in all this drabness
there is a light shining
in me
that refuses to be put out.

Lead me to your light, Lord,
and thanks.

Bewilderment

Lord,
there are days
when I'm not sure how I feel.

I'm not particularly happy
and I'm not exactly sad.

I feel I need
to talk to a friend,
to be near a friend.
Lord, are you the friend I need?

I think I have something
to say to you,
but I don't know what it is.

Maybe I should ask you
for something,
but I don't know
what I need.

I only know
I do need someone
and I think it's you.

Be with me Lord,
and fill my need.

Braces

Lord,
you're lucky
you never had to wear
braces and headgear.

Some days
all I can think about
is how much they hurt.

Other days
what hurts are the
kids who make fun of me.

I really need your help, Lord.

I need patience
to stand it until they come off.

I need hope
to remember that they really *will*
come off.

I especially need love
so I can grow a little
and not waste too much time
complaining.

Since you care about
every hair that falls
from my head,
I'm certain you won't forget
about my teeth.

Thanks, Lord.

Weariness

I don't feel like
helping anybody today, Lord.
I am really tired
of thinking about what others need.

Today *I*
need some help.
Why do I have to worry
about all the problems
of others?

I feel I want to enclose me
inside myself
and not even think
of anyone else.

But every time
I get all wrapped up
in me
I feel uncomfortable
because I feel you
looking at me.

I hear you say
    "Come to me
    and I will give you rest.
    Why are you struggling
    all alone?"

That's a good question, Lord.
Why do I carry this load
all by myself?

Here's all of it, Lord.
I need you.

Working

God, our Father,
your Son Jesus
told us not to
be anxious
about our problems.

He said we should ask you
for what we need
in his name
and you will give it
to us.

I'm not happy with my job
and I'm not sure
what to do about it.

Please show me your power,
and help me find a job
that will honor you
and enable me to use
my talents and abilities,
and let it be good news for everyone.

I ask this in the name of Jesus.

Amen.

Dieting

Lord,
thank you
for giving me life.

I want to
look and feel
as great as I can,
but somehow
my appetite
keeps getting in the way.

Please take away
my craving
for too much
food and drink.

Make me *believe*
that I don't *need*
all I take in.

Perhaps if I have less
someone who really needs it
can have more.

Without your help
I can't do it.

With your help
I can be
the slimmer me
I should be.

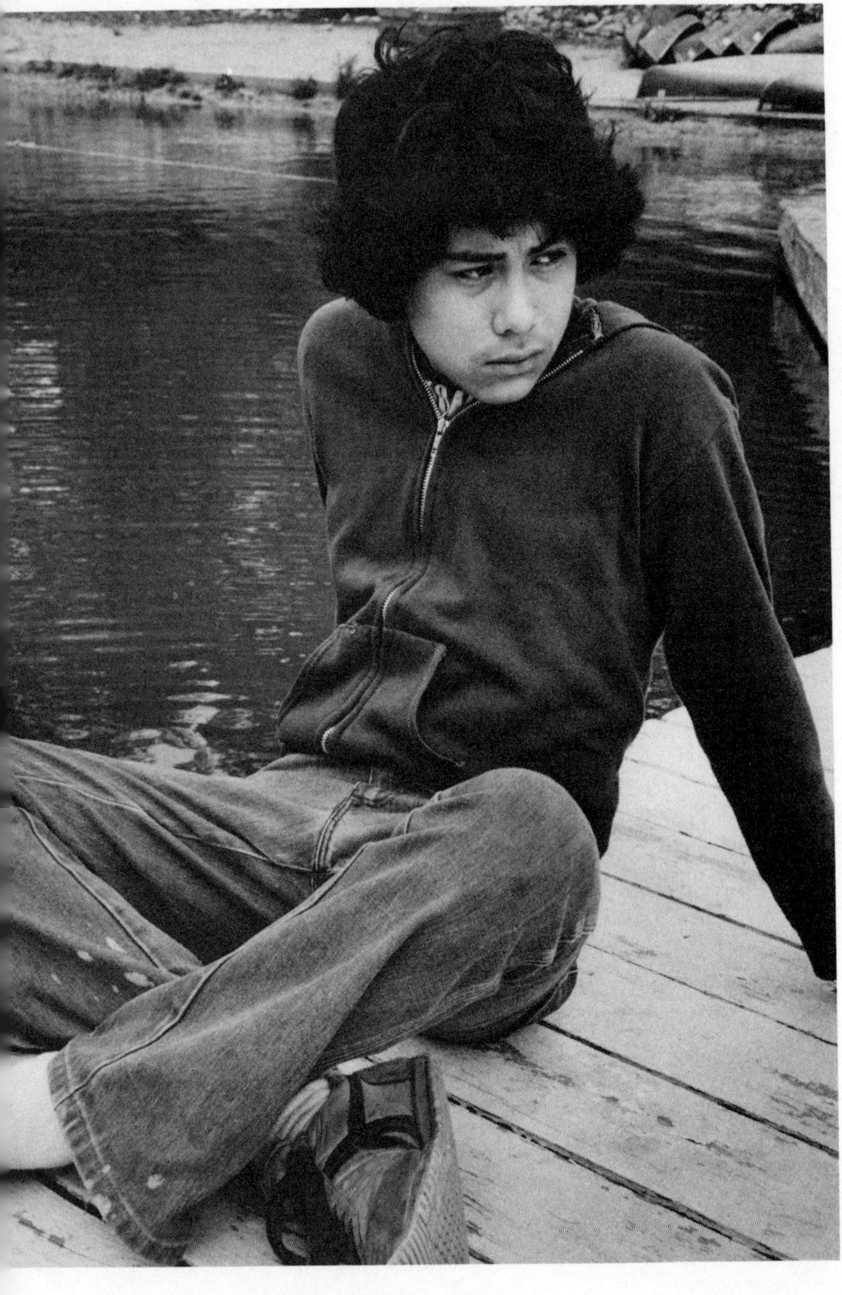

Moods

Loving Father,
there's a part of me
I don't like or understand.

Why do I get into such moods?

Good moods make things
look good but
the bad ones weigh me down.

Sometimes
it seems I doubt myself
when bad moods come;
or do bad moods come
because
I doubt myself?

And when I doubt myself
I lose faith in those
around me.
You too, God.
Then I really let you all have it.
Either a blast of words
or a miserable face.

When I'm wrapped up in me, Lord,
put me face to face

with a new kitten
or a fresh rose
or the wonder of a snowflake
or someone who needs me.

Something or someone
to remind me
that I am loved
and alive
and needed.

Thanks, Father.

Loneliness

Father,
there are many ways
to be miserable,
and loneliness
is one of them.

I can be right in the middle
of a group of people
and feel alone
or ignored
or without friends.

Sometimes I feel alone
because I choose not to follow
what everyone else is doing,
and sometimes that choice
even makes me feel guilty.

Maybe the worst loneliness
of all
is to be far away
from those I love.

Help me feel your presence
when I'm lonesome, Lord.

Don't let my loneliness
set me apart, but
help me bridge my sadness
by reaching out to someone else
who's lonely.

Father, thank you for caring.

Worry

You have a lot of patience, Lord.

We tell you our troubles
and ask you for help
and immediately
begin to worry.

We worry about where
money will come from
and what people
think of us
and when our complexion
will clear up
and how we'll ever
get in shape again.

And we worry about
big things too:
aging and death and pain.

We worry because
we haven't learned
to trust you, Lord.
Sometimes I think

we'd *rather* worry
than trust you!

Heal this attitude, Lord.

Teach us how
to know you better.
Then, surely we'll
trust you.

We ask this in the name of Jesus.

Amen.

Pain

Lord, today I really hurt.

I feel I'm dragging a pain
or the pain is dragging me.

I feel heavy
and wearisome
and sad.

But I realize everything
I suffer
has already been endured by you.

Your love has transformed
everything—
even (especially) pain.

Well, Lord,
I'm not as brave and loving
as you
but I'm willing to try.

Lord Jesus, walk with me
so all of this
becomes love.

Where Can I Find God?

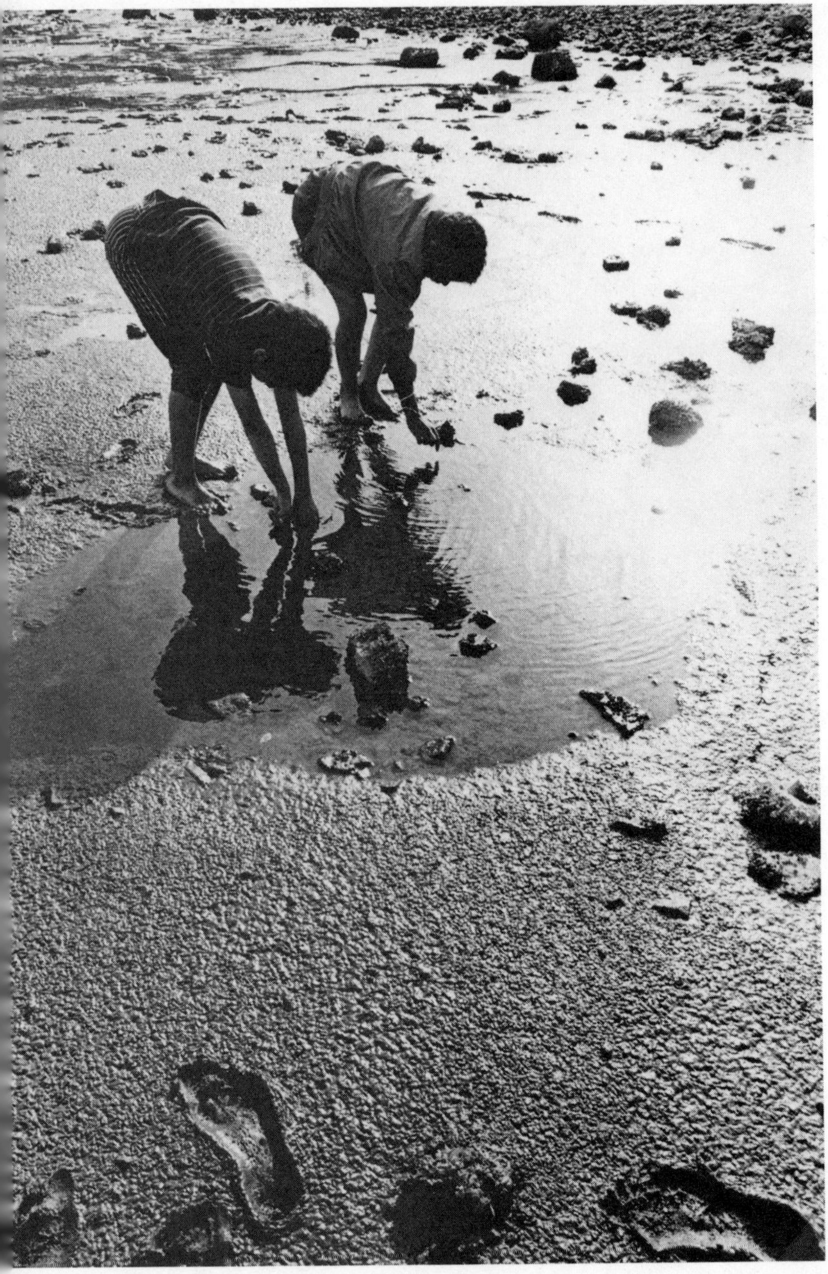

Discovery

Lord,
usually I'd say
the days are average.
Some days are great,
some I can do without,
but most of them are average.

Today
I definitely feel the day
is great.
I've made a discovery!
I've found that
I
can make a day important
or boring
or somewhere in between.

It's all in how I look at it.
And it starts
the minute I wake up:
    Is it a "yes" day
    or a "no" day?
    Will it be "love" today
    or just "me" today?
    Can I actually smile
    when I awake?
    Can I remember to say

"Lord, this day is for you,
show me how to love"?

It makes a difference.

I
make a difference.

I discovered it today.
Thanks, God.

Freeway

Lord,
there's a world
inside your world
that appears
to have no part of your love.

It's wild in the worst sense.
It's cold and concrete,
and most of the time
it's crazy.

It's called
for some reason,
"freeway."

Once wheels touch stone
I'm off to war.
And so, it appears,
is everyone else.

Why do we feel excused
from caring and fairness
just because we can
travel fast?

Gentle us, Lord,
even in the midst of the madness.
Don't leave us to ourselves
on the road, Lord.
Especially on the road.

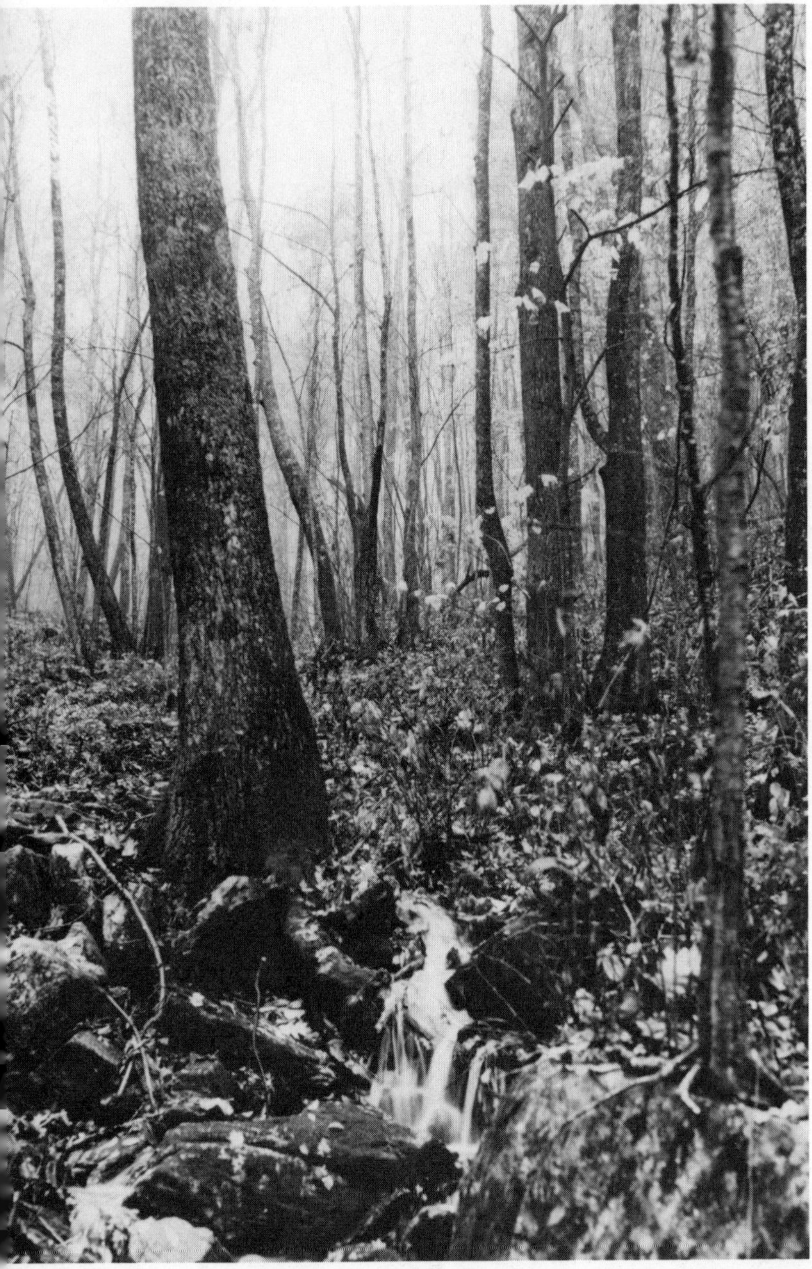

Song from the North Woods

All you clear and shimmering waters,
Praise the Lord.

All you tiny insects hovering over the water,
Praise the Lord.

All the winds in the trees,
Praise the Lord.

All you bass that avoid our lures,
Praise the Lord.

All you loons that glide and dive,
Praise the Lord.

All you chipmunks and squirrels and baby rabbits
    that eat from our doorstep,
Praise the Lord.

All you huge rocks and palisades,
Praise the Lord.

All you silent canoes,
Praise the Lord.

All you early morning fishermen,
Praise the Lord.

All you late sleepers,
Praise the Lord.

All you kind and considerate neighbors,
Praise the Lord.

All you unnamed sounds and mysterious paths,
Praise the Lord.

May this peace and stillness
   heal our noisy minds
   so that we, too, may always
praise the Lord!

Creation

God,
the whole earth
is singing out your goodness
today.

Every color
every creature
every sound
seems to be at attention
praising you.

It is so crystal clear
and whole
that it's hard to think
of anything
but your great love
for us.

And, as if the wonder
of your creation
weren't enough,
you have made us —
your people —
in your own image.

Let all this beauty
heal us, Lord.
Let it show us
who you are.

Awareness

Lord,
we have so much.
Each day is filled
with gifts that only a
loving Father like you
would think to bestow.

How do I have the nerve
to complain
about the way things are?

It isn't as though
we've earned your gifts,
because all that we have
comes from your great love.

We're spoiled, Lord.

We expect your goodness
and it's always there.

From this moment on
I want to wonder
at your constant love.
Help me never to take you
for granted.

Backyard

Loving Father,
I find your love
in the most amazing places.

Raking in spring
is an ordinary job
and pulling back layer after layer
of dead, black leaves
from a wildflower garden
is worth the effort
when looking for signs of life
underneath.

But then to hit ice!

It made the job seem foolish
until I saw your sign of
reassurance:
a bright, green, healthy vine
stretching out beside
the ice.

Thanks, God.
Help me to keep
finding your love
in my own backyard.

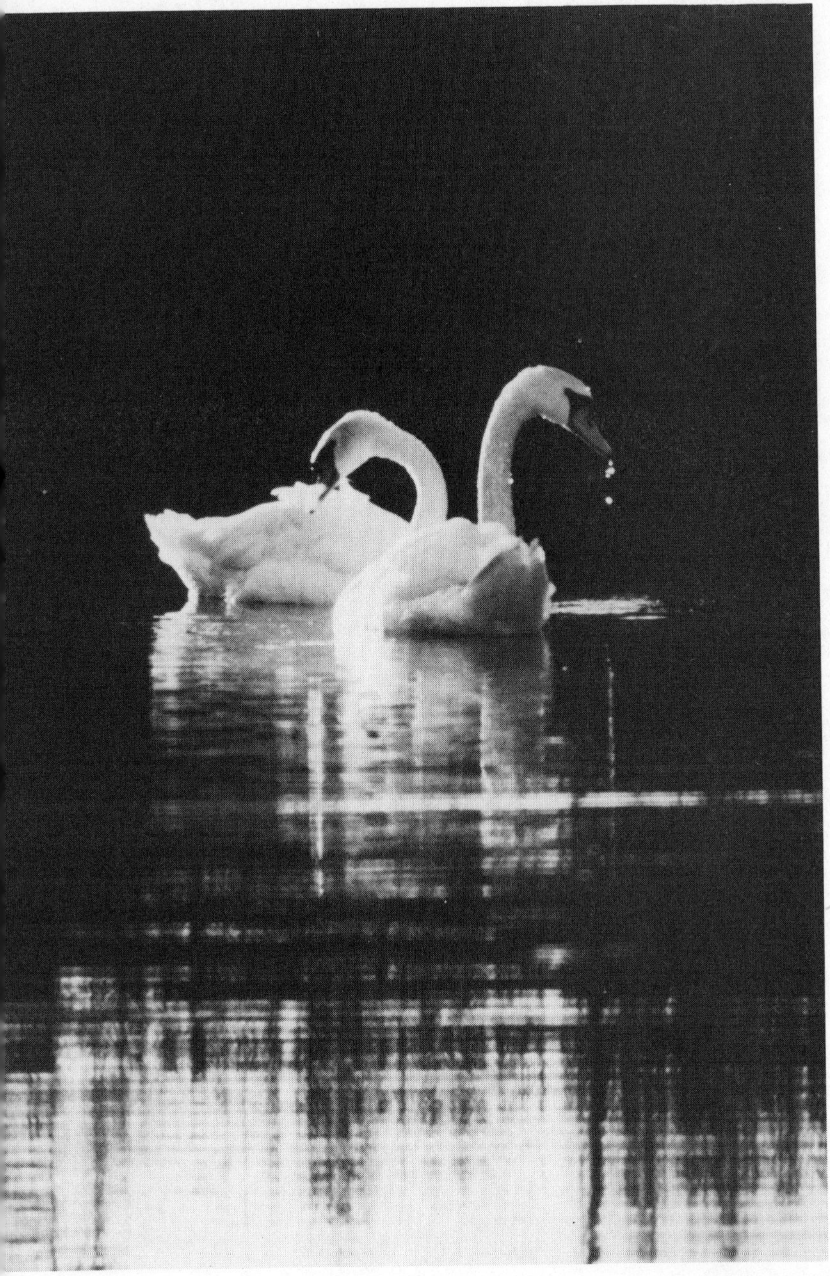

Color

Lord, our God,
I believe
you must have created
color
to tell us about yourself.

I can clearly see your glory
in a brilliant red cardinal
suddenly emerging
from a fir tree
right outside my window
on a winter day.

I feel your personal touch
in providing us with a lake
full of white swans
in the heart of the cement and steel
city.

I realize your love of simplicity
in the reds and purples and whites
of huge petunias
trailing from a single
window box
in a long row of
dull, gray apartments.

I am amazed
at your love of variety

in the shades of people
and the clothes they wear.

Semaphores teach me about
your patience;
soft, furry pets remind me that
I find comfort and trust in you.

Even gray hair
has its message!

Color is your love-gift to me, God.

Teach me to look for you
very carefully.

And thanks.

St. Therese

The little ones, Lord,
hear your secrets.

Those who love simply
and simply love;
those who trust
without complications,
without asking why,
simply expecting
all
from you
and receiving all
from you,
tireless
in seeking your will,
startling others
by their strength
to carry it out.

Pray for the rest of us,
you saints
who are utterly
loving and simple
and powerful
in God.

Search

God,
to say you are everywhere
is too general for me.

Many of your people
find you easily
in nature.
And I do too.

But I've discovered
I can find you
wherever I look
for you.

Not only at worship,
but also at baseball games.
Not only when dreams come true
but also when things
don't go the way I plan.

You are present
not only when we share
our clothes and food and money,
but maybe even more
when we struggle

to change attitudes and traditions
that keep so many needing
clothes and food and money.

You are with us
in the dull and in the exciting.
I hope you are present even in politics.

Help us in our search
for you, God.
We need you.

Death

Lord,
you know how it feels
to lose someone you love
in death.

You know
how the sadness inside
is so heavy
that there isn't room
for any other feeling.

Death
seems so final....

Yet, because I believe
you are Lord of Life,
all of us will be
new again
with your life
and your love.

Please heal
the ache inside me.
Because I believe
in your dying and rising
help me to realize
now
how much life
there is in
death.

Where in the World Are We Growing?

Risk

Lord, I'm getting the message.
I've decided my ideas
about you
are much too complicated.

Why do I keep thinking
you give me
unending lists
of dos and don'ts?

Actually, what you say
is "Love"
and "Forgive."

I'd like to learn
to risk
being that simple.

I'd like to risk being
a loving and
forgiving person.

But I know for sure, Lord,
I can't do it alone.

Heal the selfish me
so I can risk
love and forgiveness.

Trust

God,
some things are too much
for me.

I don't know how
to deal with this problem.
I don't have any answers.
I'm not even sure of the questions.

I do know
that at last
I can admit
I don't know what to do.

I am able to turn this over to you.

Lord, I trust you.
Here's my problem. . . .

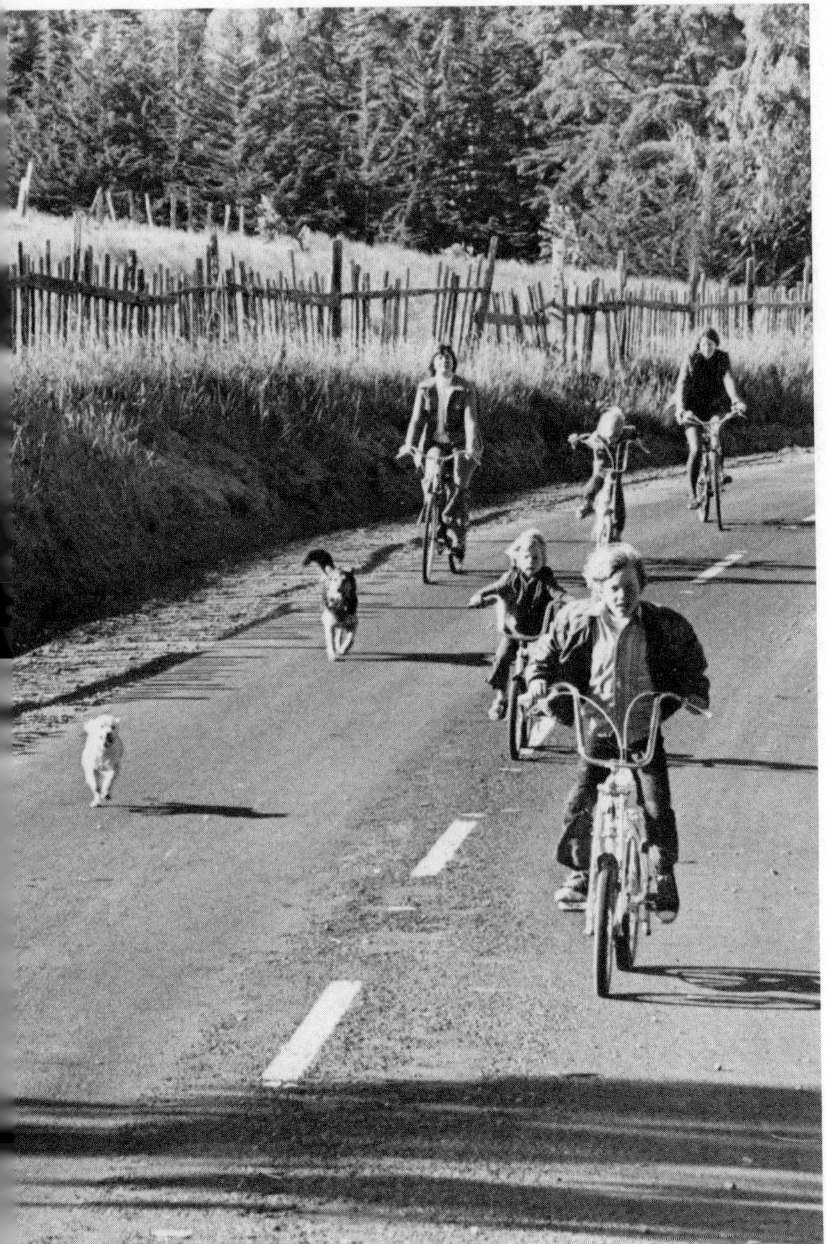

Family

Father,
thank you for giving me
a special way
to love and to grow—
being part of my family.

Sometimes
I don't like to admit
that I need them,
but I know deep down
they are a gift
from you to me.

I know this because
my family doesn't love me
for what I have or do
but, like you,
they love me because I'm me.

Like you, they even love me
when I'm mean and ugly.
Often when things get tough
they're my only friends,
maybe just by being there.

Forgive us for the days
when we grate on each other.
Fill those hard and empty times

with sharing and respect
and especially the gift of a
good laugh.

Help us to surprise each other
with a new sense of
understanding and forgiveness,
so that our family love
can reach out to touch those
without love.

Thank you for cherishing us, Father.

Rush

Slow me down, Lord.
I'm in a great hurry,
only I can't remember
why
except to keep ahead of
time.

I'm in such a rush
to get where I'm going
that I've forgotten
why I started out.

I want to live
with care
with love
with openness
with peace.

Settle me, Lord.
Give me roots
in you,
in your constancy
and calmness.

Make your life grow
in me.

Show me who you are
in your own time.

Choices

Lord Jesus,
I'd like to get into
the habit
of choosing you,
of saying "yes" to life
with love.

But there are so many
choices
to make each day
it gets confusing.

When I feel good about me
and those around me
it's easy to smile
and love and be helpful.

But those days
when I'm not sure
who I am
or how others got to be
who they are
it's hard to make
choices at all—
especially loving ones.

Lord, that's when I really
need you.
I need you to give me
a good shake,

a reminder to look at you
and your love of life
and your going out to people.

On those days
show me how to make your life
my life.

That's it, isn't it Lord?
Isn't choosing love
choosing you?

Hope

Father,
today I find it very hard
to like myself.

I feel negative and hateful.
I can't or don't want to
find anything worthwhile in me
or in the world around me.

I know this is empty thinking.

And I know, even in my confusion,
that you love me
and hold me close.

Maybe *I* don't like me
but you do,
and that should make a difference.

Help me to understand
that because you made me
I am a wonderful person.

Because you made me
I like me.
Because you care for me
I like me.
Because you love me
I like me.

Thanks, God.

Gift

Loving God,
I would like to love you
with all my heart
without thought of reward
without weakness
without ever turning away from you.

But here I am, Lord,
wanting all the right things,
giving it all to you —
then snitching back
little pieces
that I can deal with
so I feel I'm in control.

I don't like to feel helpless.

But at this moment
I realize
that's when you get your work done.

Here I am again, Lord.
Take me, all of me,
the way I want to be
and the way I am.

I want you
to use me
for your kingdom.

Progress

I think I'm beginning
to understand, Lord.

You've been after me
for a long time
to see things your way.

You pursue me
constantly
night and day
trying to show me
what my life is all about.

At this moment
I see you peeling back
the layers of my stubbornness.

The stubbornness of needing
to do things my way,
of looking out for myself
first,
of thinking how powerful
I am.

I think I am afraid
you won't be enough for me
if I choose to follow you.

Now I see you are teaching me
who you are
and who I am.

Is it all because I said
"Help"?

Worship

Lord,
sometimes I wonder
why we go to all the trouble
of going to a particular place
to talk to you,
when it's easier
to talk to you at home
(if I remember).

I've tried to do
without it,
but I find I have
a need
to praise you and sing to you
and tell you my problems
along with your other people
in a place
of worship.

It's as if we need
a gathering place
greater than ourselves
to remind us
on our journey
that our destiny
is you.

We are your people, God.
Help us to be proud
to gather in your name
to tell you
how great you are.

Values

Lord Jesus,
what are we doing
with your Gospel?

Have we all gone crazy?

Instead of hungering and
thirsting for justice,
we, like unbelievers,
chase success and
material possessions
as if they were the kingdom
that comes first.

Slow us down, Lord,
before it's too late.
Show us that our obsession
with having to have more and more
while others have less and less
is wrong.

Straighten out our vision, Lord.
Help us to put our values
in order.
Before it's too late.

Who Is Jesus, Anyway?

Question
"Who do the crowds say that I am?"   Luke 9:18

Jesus,
what are you all about?

Where do I begin
to find out
who you are?

You tell us,
"If you come to know me,
then you'll know my Father also."

I'd like that.

I'd like to know you.
I'd like to know the Father, too,
and the Spirit.

I seem to know far more about
who you aren't.

I'd like the real God to stand up
and say who he really is.

I'm here, Lord,
ready to learn.

Person

"...Jesus was welcomed by the crowd; indeed, they were all waiting for him"   Luke 8:40.

Jesus, who are you?

Like us in all ways
but sin.
What are those ways?

In the Gospels, you're
a warm and feeling person.
    People follow
    when you call.
    They gather close
    when you speak.

    You listen to each one's needs.

    You reach out.
    You touch eyes and ears.
    You lay your hands on heads
    to heal.

    You scold.
    You weep
    and encourage.
    You fill with awe
    and give hope.

    You inspire joy.

Lord, don't leave us.
Be with us always.

Outdoorsman
"...Jesus sat down by the lakeshore" Matthew 13:1.

Jesus,
who are you?

In the Gospels
nature surrounds you.

> Your birth in a cave.
> Your death on a hill.
> Your stories of
>   trees and fruit,
>   flowers and birds,
>   salt and light,
>   wheat fields
>   and mustard seeds,
>   grains of sand
>   and thorny bushes.

> You pray outdoors too.
>   In lonely places —
>   deserts and hills,
>   on mountains,
>   near lakes and in boats.
>   In a garden where olives grow.

Everything your Father made
reminds you of him
and his unending love.

Jesus, you are renewed
by your Father's creation.

Renew us too.

Free
"... If the son frees you, you will really be free"   John 8:36.

Lord Jesus,
one of my favorite thoughts
of you
as a person on this earth
is that you were free.

The way you
thought of yourself
was so healthy
you could freely
be yourself.

Teach me how
to value myself
and to believe in the
Father's gifts
to me.

Heal my negative ideas and fears.

Help me to believe in you
and to believe in me
so that I can be free
to be myself.

Prayerful
". . . he went out one day into the hills to pray, and spent the night in prayer to God"   Luke 6:12.

Jesus,
it's a comfort to me
that you had
certain problems
to struggle with.

I am encouraged
that you spent long nights
trying to figure out
your Father's will,
how you could be
your best self
and make right choices.

Thank you
not only for getting through
your struggles,
but for showing us how —
through prayer.

Teach us how to struggle
with our problems
by talking them over
with the Father.

Powerful
"Full authority has been given to me..."
Matthew 28:18.

Lord Jesus,
we have a lot to learn
from your use of power.

Most of us,
like the people of your time,
expect a king
to be grand and controlling.

But you choose to use your power
to heal and teach,
to be one of us,
living as we do —
but with complete love.

You do not use your power
to force us.
Instead you share it with us
by giving us the freedom
to choose you
or to pass you by.

Jesus,
with you
we praise our Father
who has given us
all the power we need
in you.

Wondering

"My Father, if it is possible, let this cup pass me by. Still, let it be as you would have it, not as I"
Matthew 26:39.

Lord Jesus,
you taught us
how to trust
by the way you prayed
in the garden
before you died.

You knew
some terrible things
were going to happen
to you.
You must have wondered
how you would be able
to stand it.
You even asked the Father
to take it away.

You simply told him
exactly how you felt,

and through this prayer
you were able to accept his will
for you.

Teach us how to do this.

Help us to turn our dread
of what will happen
into trust
in the Father's love.

Show us that our prayer
can be a willingness to accept
what is going to happen.

Friend

"... love one another as I have loved you"
John 15:12.

Jesus, my friend,
as I grow and change
and learn to use my head
and my heart,
what I know of you
is also growing
and changing.

You truly know how to be a friend.

You don't choose friends
for what they can do
for you.

You reach out
to all persons
whoever they are and
wherever they're at.
You respect all your friends
for their own unique talents
and love them just as they are.

You especially reach out
to those who are

unpopular
and despised by others.

I have a lot to learn, Lord.

I can see I need
to be free of my selfish me
if I want to be a friend
like you.

Help me, Lord Jesus,
I need you.

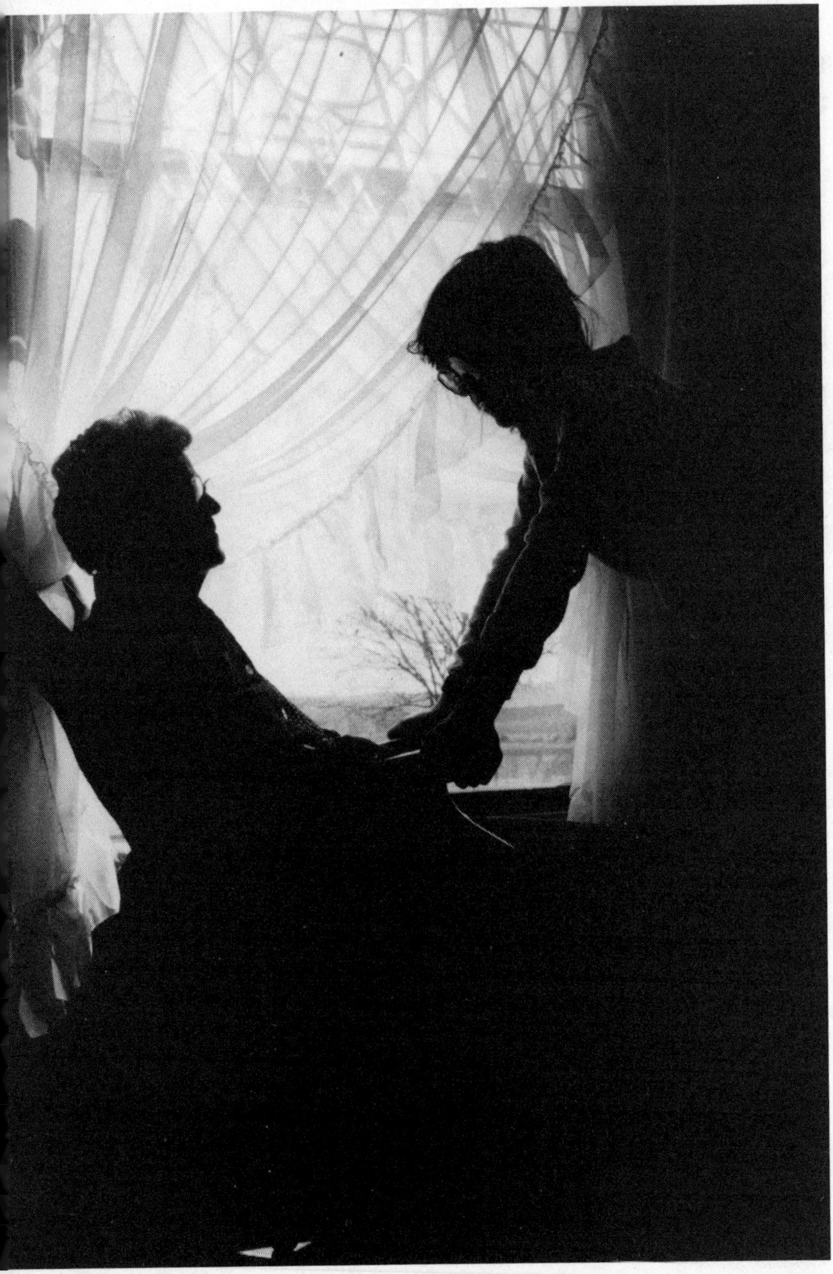

Present
"And know that I am with you always ..."
Matthew 28:20.

Jesus, I believe you are with me.

Wherever I go
you are there.

You give meaning
to every word
I speak and hear.

If I reach out
to touch the heart
of another
you are already there,
because you, Lord Jesus,
are one of us.

And because you are with us,
the ground I walk on,
the people I touch,
the words I speak and hear
can be holy.

I believe you live
and walk
and speak
and heal
on this earth
today and always.

Thank you for such love.

Successful
"I came that they might have life and have it to the full"   John 10:10.

Thanks, Jesus,
for teaching us
what success is.

Through your choices,
your courage and
your great love,
right on this earth
where we live,
you became
all that we can become.

You have given us such hope.

We each have gifts.
So did you.
But you used them so well.

You suffered and loved
and lived so fully
as a human person
that you've given us
the challenge and example
of how to suffer and love
and live fully.
Alive and whole
in God.

Thank you, Lord Jesus.
With you I'll make it too.

Does My Light Shine?

Lent

Loving Father,
during this holy time
your Son Jesus
will show us the way
to you.

Help us to pray often
so that we will
get to know you better.

Help us to fast
so that we will have more
to share.

Help us to share
our time and service
so that we will grow in love
for you
and for each other.

We ask you to
renew us
through the dying and rising
of your Son Jesus.

Amen.

Fasting

Lord, our God,
we want to return
our lives to you.

Teach us to fast
from selfishness
so that we can share
words of comfort.

To fast from food
we don't need
so that the poor can eat.

To fast from
wasting time
so that we can make time
to help others.

To fast from
laziness
so that we will be
open and waiting
for you
when you come
in all your glory.

Holy Week

Loving Father,
during these holy days
we ask you for the gift
to understand
the dying and rising
of your Son Jesus.

Change our hearts
and our attitudes
so that as we die with him
to all that keeps us
from you
we will surely live with him
in your love and glory
forever.

Amen.

Kingdom

Lord, the journey to your kingdom
is a problem for us.
We often think it's
"up there" or "out there,"
but you said your kingdom is right here,
in us, in ordinary things, today.

You said it's like
the things we touch and feel:
   a tiny seed,
   a hidden treasure,
   a silver coin,
   a beautiful pearl.

If your kingdom begins here,
then we have already arrived.
Why are we so often looking
off in the distance?

I hear you say,
   Be simple. Why do you make
   following me so complicated?
   Listen with love to my stories.
   Open your eyes.
   Hear with your ears
   and I'll show you that
   my kingdom is right where you are.

Open our hearts and our eyes and
our ears to you, Lord.
Let us recognize your kingdom
within us.

Easter

There's something new
and wonderful today, Lord,
something in the air.

It's an excitement
and a tingling
and a feeling we'll explode
with joy.

For you have truly risen, Lord.
The Father has gifted
all the world
with your New Life.

And we share in it.

Thank you for the wonder of it all.

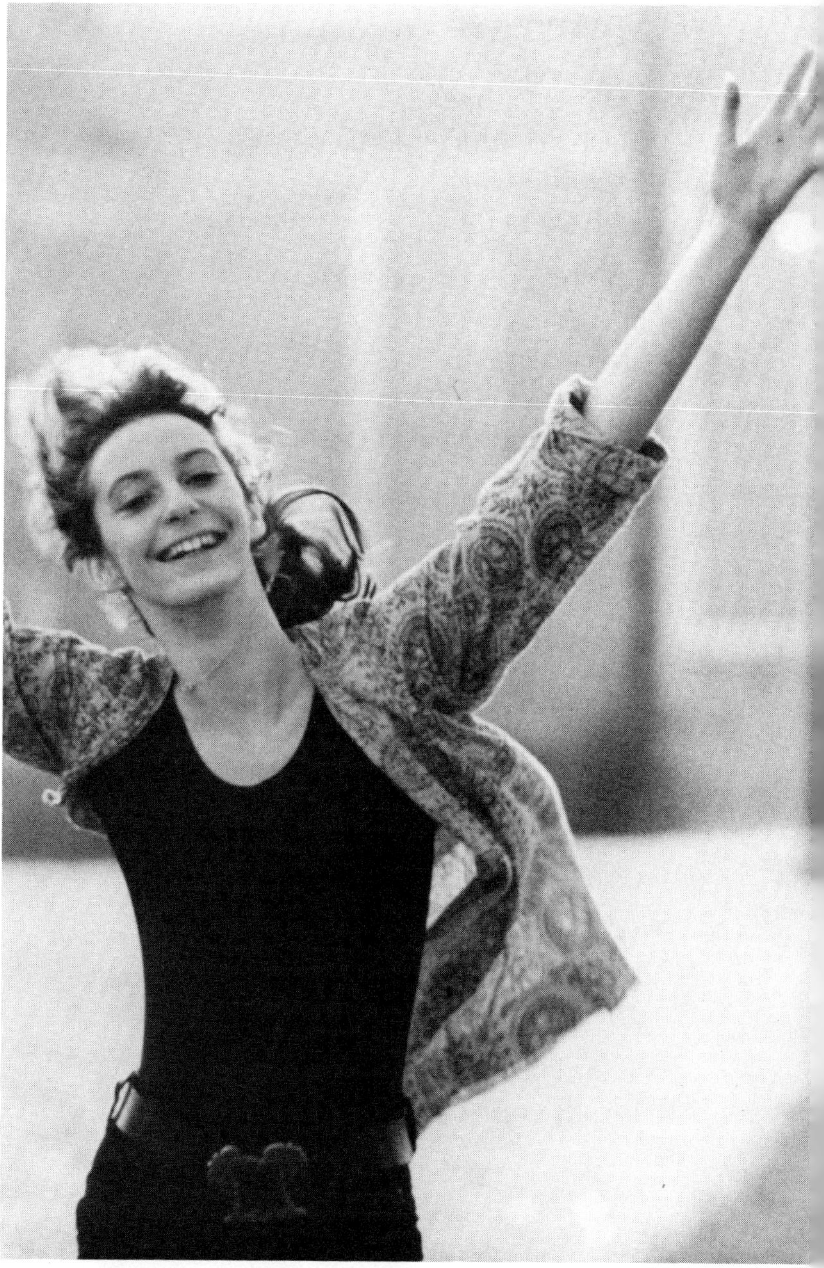

Spring

Loving Father,
these are glorious days.
I see the world filled
with your love.

The brightness of the sun
cheers us
and warms us
and reflects
how wonderful you are.

If we listen carefully
each morning,
the birds have a new song.

If we look carefully,
trees and bushes and flowers
are showing off
something green,
something new,
something never seen before
exactly like it is today.

We are surrounded
by bursting new life
and light.

Thank you
for all your care

in sharing your creation
with us.

Help us to cherish
all that you have made,
to listen
and look
and love
very carefully.

Gratitude

Loving Father,
I have everything
to thank you for,
but most of all
I am grateful
that you have
gifted me with faith.

Out of the many ways
that people believe,
you've given me
the gift of being Christian —
of believing in
the person of Jesus.

You've given me
a real person
to love
and follow.

And that real person,
one of our own kind,
is also God.

It's too much
to fully understand

such enormous love,
but I want to try.

I thank you,
I praise you,
I love you,
and I ask you
to make your gift grow always.

In the name of the risen Jesus.

Amen.

Holy Spirit

Loving Father,
as we celebrate
newness of life,
make new in each of us
your Holy Spirit,
the Spirit of Jesus.

Help us to listen
to your Spirit
when he teaches and guides us
and shows us what is
right and true.

Through the power
of your Spirit
help us to say "yes" to Jesus
and follow him with love
all the days of our lives.

We ask this
in the name of Jesus,
your Son and our Brother.

Amen.

Peace

Loving God,
thank you for life
and for the gift
to grow and change.

Peace once meant
an absence of war,
great or small,
an absence of conflict
in myself and the world around me.

But through your goodness,
I've learned that
peace is a Presence,
a fullness, a positive
sense of order
and blending together
if I look for you
in myself and in the world around me.

You've been with me always.
But now my peace is
understanding
that you are truly with me
and that you are in control
of all that is real in my life.

I renew now
my choice to follow you
and to be peace
to others as you are
to me.